A TOUR OF MID & SOUTH DOWN

To D.E.F. & BA.

The WAG numbers after each photograph refer to the
Green Collection held at the Ulster Folk & Transport
Museum, Co. Down, from where prints may be obtained.

Friar's Bush Press
24 College Park Avenue
BELFAST BT7 1LR
Published 1992
© Copyright reserved
ISBN 0 946872 52 X

Designed by Leslie Stannage Design, Belfast
Printed by W. & G. Baird Ltd, Antrim

Front cover: The Stocks, Dromore *c.* 1915 (WAG 1193)
Back cover: Castle Warders, Hillsborough Castle (WAG 3847)

A Tour of Mid & South Down

1910-35

*Historic photographs from the W. A. Green collection at the
Ulster Folk and Transport Museum.*

Jane E. M. Crosbie

INTRODUCTION TO MID & SOUTH DOWN

This tour of mid and south Down, as seen through the photographs of William Alfred Green (taken between 1910 and 1939), starts in Ballynahinch and weaves its way round the western edge of County Down, following, in parts, the course of the Bann, to the inland port of Newry. It then heads east to the seaside resorts of Warrenpoint and Rostrevor and finally swings inland and northward through Hilltown to Castlewellan.

The tour takes in a wide and disparate area including large towns and small villages; industrial and rural districts; inland and coastal settlements. However, there are common threads running through the locality. The linen industry was instrumental in the growth and prosperity of many of the towns and this led, indirectly, to the development of others as popular holiday resorts for merchants and workers alike. The railway, which developed in the mid-nineteenth century, improved communications and considerably assisted in the development of the area.

The influx of Huguenot immigrants into the county at the end of the seventeenth century introduced new methods of linen weaving. However, it was the technological innovations and developments of the nineteenth century which truly shaped the linen industry and which had such a dramatic social and economic effect on County Down. The development of power-spinning mills left a permanent mark on the landscape. The first wet-spinning mill in Ireland was set up by the Murland brothers, James and William, near Castlewellan in 1828. The introduction of powered spinning led to the development of large-scale manufacturers, primarily at Dromore and Banbridge, and then throughout the region. E. R. R. Green in "The Linen Industry in County Down" (*Industrial Archaeology in County Down,* Belfast, 1963)

notes that *"the greatest of the County Down manufacturers was John Cromie of Draper Hill, near Castlewellan"*, who employed between 2-3,000 weavers in the mid-nineteenth century.

Linen production became a major industry, not only in County Down but throughout the province. All aspects of linen production provided employment in County Down from growing flax through spinning and weaving to finishing. In the early twentieth century, when these photographs were taken, the methods used in linen production had not changed greatly since the nineteenth century and, during the first world war, linen experienced a resurgence in popularity. Although it was hit by a general post-war slump, it continued to be an important source of employment until after the second world war.

While linen was important as a primary or additional source of employment, it was not the only industry in the area. There was a long tradition of brewing in towns such as Newry and Dromore, but by far the largest source of employment in the area was agriculture. The agricultural statistics released by the Board of Trade for 1989 and 1899 recorded that 86.7% of County Down was used for agricultural purposes, almost equally divided between arable and pasture. The principal crops were oats - 97,000 acres; hay - 63,000 acres; potatoes - 43,000 acres; turnips - 20,000 acres; wheat - 9,000 acres and flax - 6,000 acres. Both beef and dairy cattle were kept and in areas such as Hilltown, where the pasture on upper slopes was rather rough, sheep were numerous. In addition many small farmers also kept one or two pigs as an extra source of income. Most towns and villages had market houses and held weekly fairs or markets and some towns, such as Castlewellan, held separate livestock and produce markets each week.

Improving systems of transport during the eighteenth,

nineteenth and early twentieth centuries, helped the economic development of the area. The Newry canal was built in the 1730s, in an effort to provide a quick method of transporting coal from Coalisland in County Tyrone to Newry. It extended 18 miles from Newry to Lough Neagh and as well as carrying cargo, between *c.*1813 and *c.*1845, there was a passenger service on the canal. The arrival of the railways in the mid-nineteenth century sounded the death-knell for the inland canal while the dock gradually declined as cargo ships got larger. However, as seen in these photographs the canal was still working, well into the first decades of the twentieth century.

Most economic activities were boosted by the development of the railways in the mid-nineteenth century. Although they were later amalgamated, various lines in County Down developed independently. The Ulster Railway line between Moira and Belfast was completed in 1847. This initially provided a great boost to local merchants and farmers as it opened up a wider market for their produce. Newry, which was already a major port and market town, had mixed experiences with the railways. An Act of Incorporation was passed on 31 July 1845 enabling the Newry and Enniskillen Railway Company to start work on a new stretch of line. The idea was to open up the port of Newry to the merchants of the west; however, the potato famine which ravaged the population in the mid-1840s almost wrecked the company before it began. It was March 1854 before the first three and and a half mile stretch from Newry to Goraghwood was opened.

Other towns and villages flourished with the arrival of the railways. Warrenpoint and Rostrevor became popular holiday destinations after a railway was opened linking them to Newry.

The population of County Down as a whole declined from 1841 onwards. In 1841 the population was 361,446 whereas by 1911, when many of these photographs were being taken, it was 204,303, a fall of 157,143. However, the main towns in the mid and south Down area witnessed a marked rise in population. Banbridge's population grew from 3,324 in 1841 to 5,101 in 1911 and 5,640 in 1837. Conversely, the population in Newry fluctuated from 11,972 in 1841 to a high of 14,808 in 1881 to 11,963 in 1911 and 12,746 in 1931. Large numbers of people left County Down from 1851-1915 and most towns had emigration agents. Another factor in the decline of population during the period 1910-39 was, of course, the Great War (1914-18).

The fine scenic photographs of William Alfred Green show a slightly sanitised view of life in the area. Many of the photographs were taken to be used as postcards or simply reflect his own interests as a member of the Belfast Natural History and Philosophical Society. However, he does illustrate many aspects of life which have now disappeared completely, such as the hand-loom weavers in Waringstown and Moira, and his photographs reveal the importance of the linen industry in the county.

There are two photographs which show the shop and house in Margaret Square, Newry where he was born on 10 January 1870. He moved to Belfast *c.*1895 after the death of both parents and worked for a while in his great-uncle Forster Green's establishment before training as a photographer with Robert J. Welch, the leading photographer of his day. He opened his own professional studio in 1910.

The selection of his photographs shown here reflect towns and villages which have changed over the inter-vening years but yet remain instantly recognisable. Any omissions are those of the photographer not the author.

JEMC 1992

BALLYNAHINCH, Co. Down (WAG 2698)

This panoramic view of the town was taken from the Hillsborough road. The spire of Mageradroll parish, Church of Ireland church can be seen to the right. The original church, built in 1772 by Lord Moira, had to be demolished in 1829 and rebuilt; however, the original tower and spire were retained. In the centre of the photograph is the tower of St Patrick's Roman Catholic church. The church was first built in 1807 but had to be rededicated in 1843 after being severely damaged in the storms of 1939. The tower and transept, added in 1866, were designed by W. J. Barre. The town was lighted by electricity from 1914.

SPA, near Ballynahinch (WAG 2699)

The Spa at Ballynahinch had been a resort since the early eighteenth century. The popularity of the Spa was due to the supposed medicinal properties of the waters and hundreds flocked to the area between May and October every year. Writing on 12 July 1760 Mary, Mrs Delany, noted that *"Master Price is much better with drinking the Ballynahinch waters - a chalybeate in this neighbourhood."* (*Letters from Georgian Ireland: the correspondence of Mary Delany 1731-68*. Edited by Angélique Day. Belfast, 1991). The Assembly Rooms, seen here, were built in 1840 by the Ker family (the local landlords), and were purchased by the adjacent temperance hotel in 1900. In the 1920s the Elmwood Spa hotel was owned by Mrs W. R. Flinn and advertised that it was *'One of the Finest Inland Hotels in the North of Ireland. Exquisite View; Tennis and Croquet Lawns; Sulphur and Iron Springs; Hot Sulphur Baths. Large Comfortable Rooms. Late Dinner. Adjoining the Golf Links.'* (*Ulster for your holidays.* Ulster Tourist Development Association, Limited. Belfast 1928). It was used to station troops in the second world war and is now a masonic hall.

MAIN STREET, Saintfield (WAG 3046)

Taken *c.*1910, this photograph shows Main Street taken from the Square. The majority of the buildings were built in the first half of the nineteenth century. The building on the left at the corner is Minnis Bros, Ltd, which was established in 1866. Beside it is Alexander Batton's grocer's shop. The last building on the right is McRobert's public house. This was the site of the Price family's original eighteenth century house. In 1802 the Prices (who built Saintfield House, *c.*1750) converted this into a 'commodious Inn'.

MAIN STREET, Saintfield (WAG 3042)

Taken c.1910 this photograph shows part of the upper half of Main Street. There is a pleasing mix of Georgian and early Victorian architecture; of special interest is the coach arch in the building to the left of Marshall's shop. On the left, behind the trees, is the Church of Ireland parish church which was built in 1776.

SAINTFIELD PRESBYTERIAN CHURCH (WAG 3048)

This is the first Presbyterian church of Saintfield. It was built in 1777 to replace an earlier meeting house which is thought to have been at Fair Green. In 1792, the minister, Rev. Thomas Leslie Birch, formed the first Society of United Irishmen in County Down in his manse, which he renamed Liberty Hall. Rev. Birch took an active part in the 1798 rebellion, preaching to the insurgents on the Sunday before the battle of Saintfield (June 1798) when the rebels were defeated. Two of the United Irishmen who fought and died at the battle are buried in the graveyard. They were John Lowry of Ballyhorran and James McEwan of Ballymacreeley.

THE GUILDHALL, Saintfield (WAG 3047)

This is now the church hall of the First Presbyterian Church. In 1892 the Rev. Stewart Dickson organised a guild which professed *"to foster a healthy and stimulating fellowship, to be educational, and to afford opportunity for an exchange of views on matters religious and social." (Walk about Saintfield,* Enid Minnis, Saintfield, 1985). The Guildhall was opened on 20 November 1901 to accommodate all the members of the Guild. It also functioned as a church hall.

ACADEMY SCHOOL, Saintfield (WAG 3043)

Saintfield Public School, later Academy, was built in 1824 by public subscription; however, before work began, Nicholas Price, the landlord, offered to enlarge and remodel the building at his own expense. The first prinicipal was Rev. James Phillips of Glasgow, and pupils were given classes in Hebrew, Greek, Latin, some modern European languages, mathematics, English and writing.

A combination of lack of official funding and the growth in National Board Schools meant that Squire Price's aspirations to create the 'Eton of Ulster' came to nothing and the school closed in 1837. The new national school opened in the building in 1850. In 1921 it was owned as a private residence by S. H. Kingham.

SAINTFIELD PARISH SCHOOL (WAG 3041)

This charming single storey building was built in 1835 for use as the parish school. In the 1830s there were six schools in Saintfield town, serving a population of between 1,053 in 1831 and 909 in 1841. By 1921 the population had fallen to 533 and there was one school, a national school with six teachers. The building was used as an Orange Hall for a while before the Orange Lodge moved to the market house. It then became private property.

RAILWAY STREET, Saintfield (WAG 3044)

This is in fact Station Road. The Belfast and Co. Down Railway Co. opened a station in Saintfield on 10 September 1858. The line from Belfast went on to Downpatrick and Ardglass. It did not have too great an impact on the town. Indeed Col. M. C. Perceval-Price in his article "Saintfield Parish under the Microscope" (published in *"Saintfield Heritage: a publication of the Saintfield Heritage Society.* Newcastle, 1982) expresses the opinion that it *"had little impact on the town's development except to hasten the demise of the old Downpatrick stage-coach service which for years had called at Saintfield on its journeys to and from Belfast".* The station was closed on 16 January 1950. On the left of the photograph is Daniel Murray's spirit dealers establishment.

FAIRVIEW, Saintfield (WAG 3045)

This area, seen here from the Ballynahinch road, has had a variety of names from Cow Fair to Fairview, and it was in this area that the first houses were built. Saintfield held a horsefair once a month which was considered to be one of the best in Ulster. The children in the centre of the photograph appear to be standing in and beside an animal pound.

HILLSBOROUGH (WAG 2467a)

Taken *c.*1930 this shows the market square. On the left of the photograph is the courthouse. There has been some discussion about the exact date of this building. However, it is known that it was erected in the last decades of the eighteenth century, probably replacing an earlier market house. The other houses seen here are a beautiful mix of late eighteenth century and early nineteenth century buildings. On the right may be seen the premises of John Houston, Spirit Dealer.

WAR MEMORIAL, Hillsborough (WAG 2469)

The war memorial in Hillsborough stands in front of the gates to St Malachy's Church of Ireland church. It was erected in 1920/1 by public subscription and takes the form of a celtic cross. St Malachy's was built between 1760-74 and was paid for by Wills Hill, 1st Marquis of Downshire. The original seventeenth century church was in very bad repair and the new church, although larger, used some of the old foundations. The discovery, in the church grounds, *c.*1800, of a habit-clad skeleton, clutching a silver chalice, leads one to suspect that an earlier ecclesiastical establishment existed in this vicinity.

GOVERNMENT HOUSE, Hillsborough (WAG 2471)

Hillsborough Castle was planned by the 1st Marquis of Downshire, Wills Hill, but was not completed until 1797, four years after his death. Sir Charles Brett, in the Ulster Architectural Heritage Society's survey of Hillsborough (1974) describes it as *"a pleasant if not very imposing two-storey, rather rambling, ashlar mansion-house."* The castle was improved and augmented in the mid-1800s and was bought by the government in 1924 to be used as the offical residence of the governor of Northern Ireland.

LAKE AND CHURCH, Hillsborough (WAG 2468)

The lake lies in the large park which formed part of the Downshire demesne. When Mrs Delany (a prolific letter writer and the wife of the very Rev. Patrick Delany, Dean of Down), visited Hillsborough on 1 October 1758 she noted that *'Lord H., Mr Bayly and I walked round the improvements, a gravel path two Irish miles long, the ground laid out in very good taste, some wood, some* *nurseries; shrubs and flowers diversity the scene; a pretty piece of water with with an island in it, and all views pleasant." (Letters from Georgian Ireland; the correspondence of Mary Delany 1731-68*, edited by Angélique Day, Belfast 1991). Visitors to Hillsborough today can still share these early improvements.

OLD CASTLE, Hillsborough (WAG 11)

The first fort on this site was built by Peter Hill in the 1630s and was remodelled and strengthened by his brother Arthur who was appointed Hereditary Constable of the Fort of Hillsborough on 20 December 1660. On 19 June 1690 King William stayed at the fort and it was here that the *Regium Donum* was signed, which granted money to the ministers of the Presbyterian Church in Ireland. The fort was further improved by the 1st Marquis of Downshire in the mid-eighteenth century. In 1921 there were 16 castle warders and a drill instructor, Sergt-Major Jas. H. Crane. It was given, by the family, to the people of Northern Ireland in 1959.

CASTLE WARDERS, Hillsborough Castle, (WAG 3847)

Sir Arthur Hill and his descendants as hereditary constables of the fort of Hillsborough were allowed to enlist 20 warders to the fort. In the nineteenth century they were 'on parade' every Sunday at the church. Richard Hayward in *In praise of Ulster* recounts that *'It used to be quite a sight to watch the old Warders of the Fort attending church parade every Sunday in their quaint uniforms of the seventeenth century, and it made me sad to notice that every time I witnessed their assembly there seemed to be fewer of the musical-comedy-like veterans."* In the 1930s Lord Downshire decided to stop recruiting new warders. Only 1 warder now survives.

HAND-LOOM WEAVER AT WORK, Moria
(WAG 285)

Hand-loom weaving had always played an important part in the overall linen production of the area. Although most linen production was centred in large factories, by the time this photograph was taken in the early twentieth century a number of people continued to earn a living from home production. In the Moira area the hand-loom weaving trade continued up until the mid 1950s. The population in the first decades of the twentieth century was approximately 550, of whom the majority were farmers.

DRAWN-THREAD WORK, Moria (WAG 286)

With so much linen being produced in the area, many companies, both local and from Scotland, employed agents in the villages and small towns of County Down to subcontract women to do fine-needle work. This provided many households with a useful second source of income. The finished linen products, with intricate and laboriously worked detail, found their way into the top households in Europe and farther afield. In 1921 Moira boasted three linen companies: Charles Bann Lavery, weaving and white work; H. H. Menzie, hemstitching and finishing; and Fredk McCaw & Co., Moira Hemstitching Co., as well as the Misses B. & N. Grant, agents for whitework.

THE SQUARE, Dromore (WAG 636)

The market house, seen on the left, was built in 1886 and was one of the last market houses to be built in Ireland. The original Georgian market house, erected in 1732, was pulled down to make way for the new edifice - Victorian town planners were not always conservationists or improvers. Just visible to the right of the market house is 'R. J. Poots & Co. Posting establishment, wholesale and retail grocer, spirit and seed merchant.'

CHURCH STREET, Dromore (WAG 637)

Taken from the top of Church Street, looking towards Market Square c.1916, this photograph shows several points of interest. On the right is the post office which was run by Mrs Mary McCleery. Note the horse and trap on the left; today, with our motorised transport, it seems very narrow.

OLD CROSS, Dromore (WAG 629)

This cross is believed to have been erected by St Colman when he founded the abbey in Dromore in the ninth century. The letters patent issued by James I mentions *"a great stone cross"* beside the church of Dromore. In the mid-nineteenth century its ruins lay near the market house and for many years its base was used as a stand for the stocks. It was reconstructed in 1887 in the grounds of the cathedral. St Colman's stone pillow is also kept in the cathedral.

CATHEDRAL CHURCH OF CHRIST THE REDEEMER (WAG 628)

The cathedral church in Dromore was built on the site of the original abbey in 1661, by Bishop Jeremy Taylor at his own expense. It was remodelled and enlarged in 1808, again at the expense of the bishop, Thomas Percy. It was further enlarged in 1868 and 1899 when a new chancel and apse and broad north aisle were added. Both Bishop Taylor and Bishop Percy were leading churchmen in their day. Jeremy Taylor wrote *Holy Living* and Samuel Johnson said of Bishop Percy that *"A man out of whose company I never go without having learned something. I am sure that he vexes me sometimes, but I am afraid that it is by making me feel my own ignorance."* When the improvements were made in 1868 Robert Harrison discovered five human skulls in a vault which were thought to have belonged to Bishop Taylor, his wife and three other bishops.

ST COLMAN'S ROMAN CATHOLIC CHURCH
(WAG 633)

St Colman's was built between October 1871 and September 1873, mainly through the perseverance of the Very Rev. William McCartan. The original church was demolished to make way for the new building. During the period of the penal laws the Roman Catholics in the district worshipped at the area known as the Mass Forth. After the end of the penal laws the Church of Ireland bishop, Thomas Percy gave this site to the Roman Catholic Community to build a church: however, when Fr McCartan was appointed parish priest in 1859 (according to J. F. Mulligan in *A Ramble through Dromore,* 1866, reprinted, Dromore 1991.) *"he found the chapel a mere hovel and the Parochial Schools in ruins. He at once took steps to improve this aspect of affairs."*

DROMORE CASTLE (WAG 635)

It is thought that this is the tower house which William Worsley built in 1610 to protect his brother-in-law, Bishop John Tod, who was elected Bishop of Dromore in 1606. In his *Guide and Directory to county Down* (1888) G. H. Bassett reports that *"The Castle of Dromore, now owned by Mr Wm. Harrison of Ballaney, is only a fragment in comparison to what it was. Mr Wm. Clarke, whose place of business is near it, declares that not a stone has dropped out in 25 years."* Although there is no sign of Mr Clarke the establishment of J. W. Ballintyne's painter, paperhanger and glazier may be seen on the left.

COWAN HERON HOSPITAL, Dromore
(WAG 634)

The Cowan Heron hospital was designed by Henry Hobart who was the founder of Hobart and Heron, architects, and the architect of many of Dromore's finest buildings, including the Ulster Bank in Church Street, built in 1920. The hospital was erected in 1898 at a cost of £7,000 which was paid by William Cowan Heron, D.L., J. P. Until his death at the age of 97 on 7 June 1917, he regularly met the cost of improvements and repairs for the hospital. He also provided shares in railway and harbour stock which paid a dividend of several hundred pounds annually towards maintenance. The future of the hospital has recently come under threat.

THE BISHOP'S PALACE (WAG 632)

The bishop's palace was built in 1781 by Bishop William Beresford. It was improved and the grounds were laid out by Thomas Percy, Bishop of Dromore, 1782-1811. The palace was sold to a James Quinn in 1842 when the see was absorbed by Down and Connor. In 1883/4 it was sold to the Jesuit Order for £8,200, who renamed it Loyola House and ran it as a novitiate house. However, the novitiate house only operated for four years and closed in 1888. During those four years one of the more famous visitors to Loyola House was Gerard Manley Hopkins who wrote two sonnets, *'Tom's Garland'* and *'Harry Ploughman'* while staying there in 1887. The Jesuits retained possession of the property until January 1918 when it was sold for £8,840. The house is now in ruins.

THE STOCKS, Dromore *c.*1915 (WAG 1193)

The stocks were first erected in Dromore *c.*1805. John F. Mulligan in *A ramble through Dromore* (Dromore 1886, reprinted Dromore 1991), says that they *"are probably as good a specimen of this instrument of punishment as could be found in the United Kingdom."* Prior to being moved to their present position outside the market house (1910) they were, for a time, on the base of the old cross, before it was reconstructed in the grounds of the cathedral (1887). Of interest are the posters, especially to the left of the R.I.C. officer, the *'Aliens Restriction Order'* and in the top right, the election poster *'Vote for William Graham, who belongs to no clique.'*

THE VIADUCT, Dromore (WAG 630)

The viaduct over the Lagan at Dromore was built in 1860/1 by the Banbridge Lisburn & Belfast Railway Co., which was later absorbed by the Great Northern Railway. It was designed by Thomas Jackson and although it has not been used since 1956 it is still visible today from the Dromore by-pass, a magnificent monument to our railway past. Thomas Jackson is perhaps best known as the architect of St Malachy's Church, Belfast.

THE GRANGE, Waringstown (WAG 1006)

Now known as the Grange, this house was built in 1698 and is shown here with its original thatched roof. The Ulster Architectural Heritage Society's survey (1979) of Waringstown remarks that it is *"one of the few remaining examples of a type once common in the English settled Lagan valley."* In his book *Recollections of an Ulster Archdeacon* (Belfast, 1934) the Rev. E. D. Atkinson, a former rector of Waringstown, recalls a visit to the parish by the then Bishop of Chhota Nagpur, Dr Whitley. He expressed a desire to see some of the weavers at work to compare their methods with those of the locals in his diocese in India. Rev. E. D. Atkinson felt that Bishop Whitely thought of Waringstown as something of a primitive backwater and was delighted to recount. *"In the centre of the cloth was displayed an elaborate coat of arms. The Bishop ... enquired who the cloth was for? and was much surprised on receiving the reply - 'The Governor-General of India'!"*

WARINGSTOWN (WAG 1000)

Waringstown was originally called Clanconnell and was purchased by William Waring in 1697. It was his son Samuel who, having become interested by the techniques in Holland and Belgium, introduced linen manufacture to the town. The cottages in the main street were all occupied by weavers and their families. Atkinson, writing about the town of the turn of the century, remarked that *"At that time (1900) almost every house had its weaving shop attached with two or three looms."* A great many of these thatched cottages were knocked down in the mid-1960s.

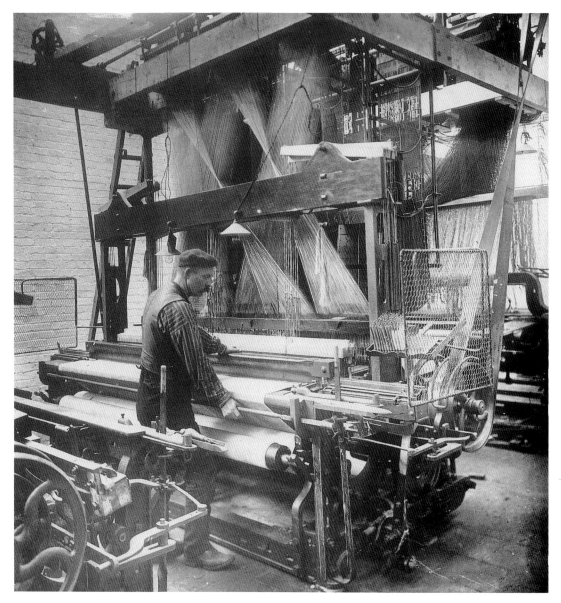

DOUBLE DAMASK WEAVING AT WARINGSTOWN (WAG 1007)

Although many weavers worked from home there were several factories which provided employment in the town. In 1921 there were two damask manufacturers in the town, William Harvey of Anaghanoon and Samuel Pennington & Sons. Damask tablecloths, with their attractive and intricate inlaid patterns, were manufactured in Waringstown and dispatched all over the world.

DOUBLE DAMASK NAPKIN POWER LOOM, Waringstown (WAG 1008)

The linen industry was a great source of employment for women. As well as working in the factories they also worked in their own homes, doing fine needlework and finishing the woven material. The napkins and tablecloths were run off in a long strip which was caught and held in the netting at the side of the loom. It was then cut to the appropriate size and finished elsewhere.

PUNCHING PATTERN CARDS FOR DOUBLE DAMASK WEAVING, Waringstown (WAG 1009)

The designs for the inlaid pattern in the heavy double damask were drawn by designers, either freelance or employed exclusively by the larger weaving factories. The man pictured here would then transform the hand-drawn design into a series of holes on a card which was used in the power loom to create the finished pattern. The skill of these craftsmen was remarkable.

SCARVA, County Down (WAG 2477)

Scarva was one of the villages on the main line of the Great Northern Railway. The Church of Ireland church, which can be seen in the centre of the photograph, was built in 1850 on the site of an ancient castle. When a lake in this vicinity was drained in the early eighteenth century numerous ancient artifacts were discovered including spearheads, brazen swords and basaltic battle axes. According to Shaw's *Guide to Carlingford Lough* (London, 1877) a canoe carved out of a solid trunk of oak was dug up in 1796. Scarva is perhaps best known as the venue of the Sham Fight, commemorating the battle of the Boyne, which is held on the demesne of Scarvagh House on 13 July each year.

MAIN STREET, Banbridge (WAG 2997)

Banbridge developed around a bridge constructed over the river Bann in 1712. It was an important staging post on the main Belfast-Dublin road. The road was very steep as can be seen on either side of The Cut. The road was levelled in 1832/4 and the bridge constructed at a total cost of £19,000. The clock tower on the left belongs to the market house which was constructed on its present site in 1834 at a cost of £2,000. The original market house was in the centre of the road, where the bridge now stands. The bridge was rebuilt in 1885, widening it from 23 feet to 47 feet.

SOLITUDE, Banbridge (WAG 2727)

The river Bann has long provided a source of income for the people of the area. As well as the usual utilisation of the river for power and the linen industry, the Bann was also famous for its fresh-water mussels and their pearls. G. H. Bassett in his *County Down guide and directory* (Dublin, 1886; Belfast, 1988) states *"a species of mussel, very large in size, throve well in its (the Bann's) waters, especially in the vicinity of Banbridge, and produced pearls abundantly. As an article of food it gained popularity only among the peasantry, for the reason that it required very high flavouring to make it palatable. The pearls were of a pale, brownish hue, and resembled those found in England and France. In the last century [the eighteenth] the fishery had dwindled to merely nominal proportions and now an occasional shell, taken from the bed of the river serves to maintain an interest in the subject among the people of the town and district."*

MOYALLON HOUSE (WAG 3251)

The townland of Moyallon near Banbridge, was given to a group of English members of the Society of Friends in 1685. The meeting house was built in 1723. The original Moyallon House which dated from the early eighteenth century was destroyed by fire *c*.1845. Jane Marion Wakefield, second daughter of the owner Thomas C. Wakefield married John Grubb Richardson in 1853. John Richardson, a Quaker, together with his brothers had founded a linen mill (which became one of the most important in Ireland) and in 1845, set up the planned village of Bessbrook, providing his workforce with good housing and schools. In 1858 the Wakefield-Richardson family moved to Moyallon and, so we are told by his daughter Jane Marion Richardson in *Six generations of Friends in Ireland (1655-1890)* (London, 1894) *"enlarged a house and made it a residence . . . remodelling and beautifying the grounds."* It is unclear whether this refers to the existing Wakefield residence or another house. John G. Richardson died in 1891 having turned down a baronetcy in 1882 for his charitable works, after he had devoted his life to his childhood ambition to *"care for the welfare of the people around him."* The figures on the steps are members of the family.

BRIDGE OVER THE BANN AT MOYALLON
(WAG 2482)

The river Bann, along with the Lagan, has provided the source of the eastern part of Ulster's great linen and agricultural wealth. The banks of both rivers, together with their numerous tributaries provided fertile ground for the growing of flax while the water was used in much of the process of production from retting to providing energy for the mills.

NEWRY (WAG 3128)

This photograph, taken *c.*1921 shows Margaret Square and Hill Street. The building on the left, Kelly and Calvert 'Select Family Grocers', was originally owned by the Green family. They lived above the shop and it was here that William Alfred (the photographer) was born in 1870. His father died *c.*1887 and W. A. Green moved to Belfast where he began to work in the business of Forster Green (his great-uncle). Note the golden teapot which remained after the Greens had left.

MARGARET SQUARE, Newry (WAG 3127)

"Newry, 'The Gap of the North' and chief centre for the famous Carlingford Lough and Mourne Mountain district, is one of the most progressive and up-to-date towns in Ireland, and stands at the head of Carlingford Lough amid a wealth of beautiful scenery, equally attractive to the sportsman, health seeker and antiquarian. The town is one of the most ancient in Ireland . . ." so said the author of *Ulster for your holidays* in the 1920s. The prosperity of the town can be judged by this view of Margaret Square. In the centre background one may see Hogg's 'Cash Stores' and J. Warnock's, booksellers, which proudly advertises that it has been *'established over a century'*, while in the foreground one may see two barefooted children.

NEWRY CANAL (WAG 3479)

Canals connect Newry with both Carlingford Lough and Lough Neagh. The Newry canal was started in 1730 and took eleven years and almost £1,000,000 to build. It was thanks to the canals that Newry became an important port which served a large hinterland in both County Down and much of south-eastern Ulster. For thirty years the Quakers from Moyallon ran a passage service on the inland canal from Newry to Knockbridge. However, during the second half of the nineteenth century this and much of the canal's inland trade came under increasing attack from the railways and during the early twentieth century from improved roads and vehicular transport. In the recent past it has been largely disused; however, there are plans to restore the canal and use it for both business and leisure.

NEWRY (WAG 3625)

A view of the town taken from the ship canal c.1920. The
ship canal was opened in 1767 in order to allow ease of
passage into Carlingford Lough and the Irish sea beyond,
and another stretch was opened in 1850 connecting the
Albert basin and Victoria docks. Unfortunately maritime
developments meant that within only a few years the
ships used for international trade were too large and so
its decline began.

SHIPS AT CANAL QUAY (WAG 3480)

The *s.s. Thrushfield*, seen here was a fairly typical steam coaster which operated between Newry and the English and Scottish ports. The *s.s. Thrushfield* was built *c*.1896 for Samuel Gray who sold it in the late 1920s to Sir Thomas Wilson and Captain William Reid. Although it was used for many varieties of cargo it is likely that the coal in the barge to the right came from it. The *s.s. Thrushfield* foundered off county Donegal in 1936.

NEWRY (WAG 3421)

A regular cross-channel steamer, the *Iveagh*, was equipped for both passengers and cargo. It was one of the last passanger ships to operate between Newry, and Liverpool. One of Ireland's main exports has always been her people and Newry in the nineteenth century developed into one of the main ports of both entry to and exit from Ireland.

NEWRY (WAG 3420)

This general panoramic view of the town is taken from the south. Clearly visible are St Patrick's church which was founded 1573 by Nicholas Bagenal and rebuilt 1866, and St Mary's which was built 1819, and which contains part of the stonework from St Patrick's including a memorial to Sir Nicholas Bagenal from the sixteenth century. Also visible is the tower of the Roman Catholic Cathedral of SS. Patrick and Colman which was added in 1888. The Cathedral of SS. Patrick and Colman was built in 1829 and was the first Roman Catholic cathedral to open in Ireland after Catholic Emancipation.

NARROWWATER, Warrenpoint (WAG 307a)

Narrowater castle stands at the point where the Carlingford Lough narrows. The first stone fortification on this site was built in 1249 by Maurice Fitzgerald. The present square battlemented tower was built in 1560 by the royal government in Dublin. The author of *Black's Picturesque Tourist of Ireland* (Edinburgh, 1866) says that *"Narrow Water castle was looked upon as the key to Newry, and from its position was well calculated either for the purpose of defence or exaction of toll. It was subsequently let to a salt-manufacturer, and at a still later period used as a dog kennel."*

NARROWWATER, Warrenpoint (WAG 1693)

A rather picturesque view of the Narrowwater. The Annals of Ulster record that the Danes established a station at Narrowwater in 790 A.D. from whence they carried out raids on the nearby territory and religious establishments such as Killeavy. They remained there until the mid-tenth century when they were beaten and driven out of Carlingford Lough by Murray McNeill. There is a 'round tower' navigation marker on the shore on the right, and another buoy in the water. The yacht is an afterthought by the photographer.

MOUNT HALL, Narrowwater, Warrenpoint (WAG 3451)

Mount Hall, or Narrowwater Castle as it was later called, was designed by Thomas Duff for Roger Hall in the 1830s. The gates are opposite the old Narrowwater castle and the house is approached via a long serpentine drive. On the other side of the low wall to the left of the house there was a magnificent, ornate Italian formal garden. The author of *Shaw's Tourist's Picturesque guide to Carlingford bay and County Down* (London, 1877) was most impressed. *"The house upon its green lawn, is a noble and picturesque object; a dwelling house, indeed, but on a scale not to take away the more important idea of a castle. . . is a splendid Elizabethan mansion of cut stone ornamented with Italian turrets and battlements, and an octagonal battlemented tower at the western end, on which a flag waves."*

HAVELOCK PLACE, Warrenpoint (WAG 318)

Warrenpoint, as late as 1780, consisted of only a few fishermen's huts and two houses. However, in the mid-nineteenth century, Newry merchants obtained a government grant to create a tidal dock at the village as, prior to 1850, ships of above 150 tons could not get further up the Lough than Narrowwater. All goods had to be transported by land or, after 1849, by rail to Newry.

The boats seen here were used to ferry boats taking tourists across to Omeath on the southern side of the lough. In 1921 in the *Ulster Town's Directory* the majority of the residents listed for Havelock Place were female, presumably either spinsters or widows, although in some cases summer houses were listed in the wife's name.

CHURCH STREET, Warrenpoint, c.1910
(WAG 324)

The main shopping street in Warrenpoint was Church
Street. It was already well established at the time of the
ordnance survey of 1830. Clearly visible in the
photograph are Bridget Mallon's public house, Thomas

Cunningham spirit dealers and hardware, and McGuffin
& Sons, bootmakers and drapers. The R.I.C. officers on
the right hand corner were part of a total force of six in
the town at this time.

THE PARISH
CHURCH,
Warrenpoint
(WAG 323)
The Church of Ireland
church was built in
1827 at a cost of £900,
on a site which was
donated by Roger Hall
of Mount Hall,
Narrowwater, who
owned Warrenpoint.
The incumbent in the
1920s was Rev. T. B.
Naylor, D.D.

BEST'S ROW, Warrenpoint (WAG 325)
This shows Best's Row, now known as Queen Street, looking east to the bathing pavilion. It was mainly residential with some holiday accommodation. Note the contrast between 'modern' and old modes of transport.

WARRENPOINT.CO.DOWN.

W.A.G. 314

WARRENPOINT (WAG 314)

The advent of the Newry, Warrenpoint and Rostrevor railway in 1849 changed the way of life for the residents of the village of Warrenpoint. The railway opened on 28 May 1849 and a banquet was held at Warrenpoint with a musical entertainment headed by the 9th Hussars. R. L. Praeger, writing in 1936 in *Ulster for your holiday,* says that *"Warrenpoint, although almost surrounded by the Mourne Mountains and the Carlingford Hills, is not relaxing; in fact, it is probably the most invigorating place on Carlingford Lough."* And thousands flocked to the resort every year, their passage aided by the efficient train service, to enjoy this *'invigorating place'.*

THE SWIMMING POOL, Warrenpoint
(WAG 2651)

The swimming pool was first built in 1908; however, in 1909 it was extensively redesigned and hot salt water baths were installed. The pool, as seen in this photograph, was designed by the firm of Messrs Kay, Parry & Ross of Dublin and Westminster and built by Messrs John Dowling & Sons of Belfast. The municipal baths were formally opened on 31 May 1909 by Lord Aberdeen, the Lord Lieutenant of Ireland. *The Belfast News Letter* on 1 June 1909 reported that *"all the* *principal thoroughfares were gaily decorated with Venetian poles, bearing trophies of flags and long streamers of patriotic hues . . . the resort had all the appearance of being en fête in celebration of an event which all concerned are certain to regard as one of far-reaching importance. The weather unfortunately proved most unfavourable, for rain fell heavily throughout the day . . . but it did not dampen the ardour of the populace.'*

THE PROMENADE, Warrenpoint *c.*1910
(WAG 316)

The hopes expressed at the opening of the railway that a heavy traffic of summer visitors would develop were fulfilled and Warrenpoint was soon a popular holiday destination. The houses on the promenade and Seaview, large mid-Victorian villas and hotels, reflect the growing prosperity of the town. Most of the large houses were summer residences for the wealthy businessmen of Newry, or guest houses. Many of the visitors were day-trippers from Newry, and further afield, able to take advantage of the cheap rail fares, seen here enjoying a quiet walk along the seafront or merely people-watching. The Great Northern Hotel, owned by the G.N.R.C., is on the left of the photograph.

THE PARK, Warrenpoint (WAG 319)

The park, with its bandstand was a popular spot for summer concerts during the visiting season. The land was given to the people of Warrenpoint by Thomas Smith of Daisy Hill, Newry, and was opened in July 1907.

The bandstand, which cost £300, was made in the same year by W. McFarlane & Co. of Glasgow and was the venue for the very popular summer concerts.

WARRENPOINT FROM OMEATH (WAG 321)

A splendid panoramic view of Warrenpoint from Omeath. The tall spire in the centre of the town belongs to St Peter's Roman Catholic church, which has acted as a landmark for shipping since its erection in 1875.

A variety of ferries operated to take visitors between Warrenpoint and Omeath, a popular day trip. In addition there was a large fleet of rowing and sailing boats for hire in the town.

ST PETER'S ROMAN CATHOLIC CHURCH (WAG 322)

St Peter's was built on land bequeathed by George Ogle Godfrey of Newry in 1839-40. It was designed by Thomas Duff, the famous Newry architect. Originally it was a classic gothic church in the shape of a cross; however, in 1875 a tower and spire were added which are 144 $\frac{1}{2}$ feet high. G. H. Bassett in the *County Down guide and directory* (Dublin, 1886; Belfast, 1988) describes the addition as *"a very great change for the better."*

WARRENPOINT (WAG 2041)

Taken from Bridal Loanan this photograph shows the town from the north with the town of Omeath visible across the lough. Also clearly visible is the spire of St Peter's church. The photograph was obviously improved by the photographer as may be seen by the buildings on the right. An advertisement for the town in the 1930s extrols the virtues of *"Charming Warrenpoint. Pleasure Gardens. Concert Parties. Hot Salt Baths. Bus Tours. Pictures. Dancing. Golf. Bowls. Tennis. Bathing. Boating. Putting."*

CLONALLON CHURCH, near Warrenpoint (WAG 2646)

There has reputedly been a church on this site since the days of St Patrick. It was the burial place of the Magennis family, Lords of Iveagh, although nothing now remains of their last resting place. This church was built in the seventeenth century during the term of office of Bishop Jeremy Taylor, and was renovated in the 1870s. Clonallon was the mother church of Warrenpoint but the parishes were separated in 1825, although they are now reunited.

ROSS MONUMENT, Rostrevor (WAG 2645)

The Ross Monument was erected in 1826 to the memory of Major-General Robert Ross (1766-1814). He was a distinguished soldier and served in military campaigns in Holland, Egypt, Italy, Spain, France and, finally, America where, according to the inscription, he *"attacked and dispersed the American forces at Bladensburg, on the 24th of August, 1814, and on the same day victoriously* entered Washington the capital of the United States." While in Washington he was responsible for the sacking of the White House. The black marble slabs which adorn the sides of the monument also tell us that he *"fell victorious at Baltimore"* in 1814. The monument is a striking landmark, but now in a very unkempt state.

THE SQUARE, Rostrevor *c.*1910 (WAG 3311)

The square is one of the focal points for the local community. This photograph taken *c.*1910 shows the square looking north towards Church Street. Tourists to the town could reach it by tramway, although this was discontinued for a while during the first world war. The entry in the *Ulster towns directory* for 1921 reports

"A connection with Warrenpoint has now been renewed and M'Anulty's motor bus meets all trains for conveyance of passengers from and to the village." Prior to the first world war this service was operated by Matier's long cars.

CHURCH STREET, Rostrevor (WAG 813)

Most of the houses seen here would have been privately owned, perhaps taking in paying guests. As a result of the mildness of its climate, Rostrevor attracted visitors during the winter months as well as the summer season. The spire of St Mary's can be clearly seen above the trees.

CHURCH OF IRELAND PARISH CHURCH,
Rostrevor (WAG 811)

The Church of Ireland parish church was built at the turn of the nineteenth century. It had a new vestry added in 1864 and a new roof in 1880. On 1 January 1919 the Ven. E. D. Atkinson was instituted as rector of the parish and although he was very happy during his twelve year ministry in the parish he found it somewhat different to his previous parish of Waringstown because, as he explains in *Recollections of an Ulster Archdeacon*

(Belfast, 1934) *"Instead of a large population mainly consisting of weavers, artisans and farmers, my flock here considered of three or four substantial farmers and a certain number of small ones, some boarding-house keepers, tradespeople and servants, with almost all the residential gentry and villa folk of whom there was a very considerable number in the parish."*

INSCRIBED CROSS, Kilbroney Churchyard, Rostrevor (WAG 310)

This delightful inscribed cross is in the graveyard attached to the ruined church at Kilbroney. It is thought to date from the sixth century. Richard Hayward in *In Praise of Ulster* (Belfast, 1936) expresses the view that this cross marks the grave of St Bronach who founded the convent. It is likely, therefore, that the face is a representation of the foundress. There is another, more ornate and skilfully executed cross in the graveyard with beautiful interlacing, which is reckoned to date from the nineteenth century.

R.C.CHAPEL ROSTREVOR   WAG 812

ST MARY'S ROMAN CATHOLIC CHURCH, Rostrevor (WAG 812)

The Roman Catholic church of St Mary's was built in 1850/1 thanks to the efforts of the parish priest the Rev. Bernard Mooney. His achievement is still remembered by a plaque which reads *"Off your charity, pray for the soul of the REV. BERNARD MOONEY P.P., whose remains lie within this sanctuary. He was pastor of this parish for seventeen years, during which time this church was erected. He departed this life the 25 November, 1864, in the 63rd year of his age."* Like St Peter's in Warrenpoint, the church spire is clearly visible for miles around.

THE FAIRY GLEN, Rostrevor (WAG808)

Whereas Warrenpoint was a mainly nineteenth century development, by that century Rostrevor was already a well established town, having grown up originally around the mediaeval castle of Rory McGennis. In those days it was called Castle Roe (Rory) but during the reign of Elizabeth I the demesne was given to Sir Marmaduke Whitechurch, who changed its name to Rostrevor, reputedly after his daughter Rose who married Edward Trevor, later Baron of Dungannon. As one can clearly see from this photograph, the charming surroundings of Rostrevor made it a delightful resort.

KILBRONEY RIVER, Rostrevor (WAG 2638)

The Kilbroney river rises in the Mournes and flows into the sea at Rostrevor. Its banks have long been a popular place for residences. St Bronach founded a convent here in the sixth century and there are ruins of a church in the villiage thought to date from the ninth century. These late nineteenth century homes are known as Roxboro Place.

BEACH AND WOODSIDE, Rostrevor
(WAG 2641)

This view shows the Great Northern Hotel and Woodside Hotel. Both had been bought in 1899 by the Great Northern Railway Co. although the Woodside was resold in the 1920s. *The author of Shaw's Tourists' picturesque guide to Carlingford Bay* (London, 1877) reports of the Woodside that *"the gardens are occasionally illuminated with chinese lanterns and variegated lamps after nightfall; and 'darkness flies away' before the bright lamps produced by one of Messrs H. Wilde & Co's patent magneto-electric light machines driven by a 6 horse power engine."* There were plans in the second half of the nineteenth century to turn the quay area of the village into a ready made holiday centre complete with large promenade, parkland area, concert hall, yacht club and skating rink. Nothing was done although a skating rink was built along the side of the Woodside hotel, and a yacht club did operate, holding annual regattas. The beach, hardly appears appealing with its lack of sand, but was perfectly safe for bathing.

ROSTREVOR HOTEL c.1910 (WAG 807)

The Great Northern Hotel was the largest of Rostrevor's hotels. Originally called the Mourne Hotel it was built in the 1870s to the designs of W. J. Watson, a Newry architect. It was purchased in 1899 by the Great Northern Railway Co. and extensively modernised. The Woodside restaurant and hotel is visible to the right of the Great Northern Hotel and it too was bought by the G.N.R.C. Both hotels were widely advertised as ideal winter retreats as was the resort itself. *"Mild in winter. Rostrevor is sheltered from gales"*, from *"Ulster for your holidays"*. (Belfast, 1920). The wooded slopes of Slieve Ban made a dramatic backdrop to the hotels.

CARLINGFORD LOUGH FROM ROSTREVOR (WAG 2035)

Although not as developed as the large docks at Warrenpoint, some coal and small cargo boats did off-load at Rostrevor. The pier was built in 1795 by John Martin. Richard Hayward in *In Praise of Ulster* (Belfast, 1936) says of the town that *"Rostrevor is quite unlike any other place in Ulster and has been aptly called 'an old English village set in a Norwegian fiord'. Trees and shrubs grow down to the very beach; . . . nothing can approach this spot but the warm southern breezes."*

CLOUGHMORE (BIG STONE), Rostrevor (WAG 806)

The Cloughmore or large stone, sits on the side of Slieve Ban and visitors to it on clear days are afforded spectacular views of the surrounding district. There are two theories as to how a 30 ton granite boulder managed to get there. The first, and more mundane, view is that it was left there by a glacier during the last ice-age. The second, more romantic theory is that it was thrown there by Finn McCoul from Carlingford mountain. He was aiming at Benandonner, the Scottish giant and his great rival, who was standing on Slieve Ban at the time; he missed and Benandonner fled.

THE "NEB" OF KILLOWEN (WAG 2692a)

Most of these cottages were owned by small farmers and labourers who were often part-time fishermen. These cottages were sometimes rented out for the summer as the owners moved to small huts in the back gardens.

NORMAN KEEP, Greencastle, Co. Down
(WAG 2056)

Greencastle was built in the thirteenth century by the Anglo-Normans under de Courcy. J. B. Doyle in *Tours in Ulster: a hand-book to the antiquites and scenery of the north of Ireland* (Dublin, 1855) says that *"The Castle stands upon an elevated rock, about a quarter of a mile from the sea . . . Upon gaining the battlements a beautiful view of the Lough scenery is obtained."* In the seventeenth century Greencastle along with the rest of the kingdom of Mourne was given to Sir Nicholas Bagenal of Newry.

HILLTOWN (WAG 1706)

The Downshire Arms Hotel, seen on the left of the picture, was built *c.*1820 The present buildings are either replacements for, or improvements of, the original inn and market house which date from *c.*1765. In 1921 the Downshire Arms Hotel was owned by J. & L. Blackburn and the *Ulster towns directory* reports that Hilltown had 10 publicans and 7 R.I.C. men as residents. The car belonged to the photographer who used it as a 'prop' in many of his photographs.

RIVER BANN AT HILLTOWN (3313)

Hilltown, although lying to the north-west of the Mourne Mountains, owes its name, not to the hills in which it is situated, but rather to the Hill family (later Marquises of Downshire) who founded the town in the mid-eighteenth century. Previously this area was part of the Carquillan estate which was forfeited to the crown in 1641.

A picturesque village, Hilltown with its pleasant walks and proximity to the river Bann was a popular destination for day-trippers from the larger resorts of Warrenpoint, Rostrevor and Newcastle and the Bann,which rises in the Mournes near to Hilltown, was a popular spot for trout fishing.

CASTLEWELLAN, Co. Down (WAG 641)

G. H. Bassett in the *"County Down guide and directory"* (Dublin, 1886, Belfast, 1988) says of Castlewellan *"In beauty of situation, no town in the county can surpass Castlewellan".* The town has a commanding situation in view of the Mourne mountains, surrounded by breathtaking scenery. It was owned by the Annesley family and in 1910 the population was 819. From *c.*1920 the town had electric lights.

CASTLEWELLAN CASTLE (WAG 644)

The Annesley family who owned Castlewellan arrived in Ireland during the reign of Elizabeth I to take part in the plantation of Munster. The first Annesley in Ireland was Robert Annesley and it was his grandson, Francis, who moved to Castlewellan. The original castle was rebuilt in the 1850s by the 5th Earl Annesley in its present form. It has wonderful views of the Mournes. The grounds of the Castlewellan castle have been open to the public for over a century, initially, when the family still lived there, on a

Monday, but since the property passed into the hands of the Forestry Commission in the late 1950s almost unlimited access has been possible. R. L. Praeger in *Ulster for your holiday* (Belfast, 1936) says that the Castlewellan demesne *"is famed among lovers of trees and shrubs for the fine collection of rare species which have been brought together here, many of them now of magnificent dimensions."*

MAIN STREET, Castlewellan (WAG 645)

Castlewellan is made up of two squares and a connecting street which is very wide. The town was one of the main market centres and also the centre of linen production in the area. The prosperity of the town and its surroundings is reflected in the size and style of the buildings in the main street. The large building on the left was O'Hagan's grocers and spirit dealers and the house beside it is Andrew Tuft's, bookseller, stationer and car proprietor.

CASTLEWELLAN (WAG 646)

This is a view of the main road through Castlewellan taken from the lower square looking towards the upper square. The building which looks like a church is the market house. During the early nineteenth century weekly linen markets were held in Castlewellan. The entrance to the Annesley demesne is off the upper square. In *The town in Ulster* (Belfast, 1951) Gilbert Camblin says of Castlewellan *"Whether the town was planned as one unit; or whether the unusual layout* *resulted from two separate building schemes is not clear. It would seem that the buildings around the market house were first constructed because this portion is known as the 'Old town', while the lower half of the settlement is referred to as the 'New town'. There can be no doubt, however that the regular shape, symmetry and spacious appearance of the town are the result of carefully prepared plans . . ."*

ST MALACHY'S ROMAN CATHOLIC CHURCH, Castlewellan (WAG 647)

The Roman Catholic church is in the Lower Square or 'New town' and was built in the 1880s. The foundation stone was laid by Patrick Dorrian, Bishop of Down and Connor, in July 1880 and the church was dedicated in September 1884 by the Very Rev. V. P. Hood. All of the money, £15,000, for the church's construction was raised locally with £1,000 alone being obtained by a ladies bazaar. The church was constructed using Mageramayo granite and was designed by Messrs Heavy & Thompson, Killyleagh.

'THE PICK OF THE BUNCH', Castlewellan
(WAG 1175)

This wonderful photograph was taken *c.*1915 at the
weekly pork market which was held in the town on
Wednesdays. The pig shown here is a particularly
impressive example of the now extinct Large White

Ulster pig. The *"gentleman who pays the rent"* as pigs
were known, was an important source of cash income in
rural areas for most of the nineteenth and early twentieth
century.

ST PAUL'S CHURCH, Castlewellan (WAG 648)

Prior to the building of St Paul's church in the 1870s, Church of Ireland services were held in the market house. The new church was built on the outskirts of the town. The cost of construction (£7,000) was borne entirely by the Annesley family. Bassett's guide *County Down a guide and directory* describes it thus *"The Church of Ireland has a commanding position. The grounds enclosing it are terraced and contribute not a little to accentuate the points of architectural excellence of which it has many. It is in the Gothic style, has a handsome porch, and amost graceful spire."*

DOLLY'S BRAE, Castlewellan (WAG 3124)

One of the most striking aspects of the approach to Castlewellan from Downpatrick is the extremely straight road which passes through Dolly's Brae, on the outskirts of the town, which lies just over the brow of the hill. The car in the centre of the photograph belongs to the photographer. Dolly's Brae was the site of a famous fracas in the mid-nineteenth century.

SOUTERRAIN IN CASHEL, Loughislandreevy (WAG 1432)

"Loughislandreevy, The Little Lough of the Island. This Island is now connected with the mainland by a causeway . . . The island is partly artificial and the traces of a cashel which can be seen on it show that it was a strongly fortified place in ancient times." In Praise of Ulster (Belfast, 1938). Cashels were enclosures which were surrounded by stone walls. In some cases, such as the one at Loughislandreevy there were underground passages which opened out into chambers. The main purpose for the souterrains was security, as although cashels were built in easily defended places they were purely for living in; huts were erected and animals brought in at night.

LEGANANNY DOLMEN, Castlewellan (WAG 25)

Signs of past inhabitants of the area are scattered throughout mid and south Down. Dolmens such as this were burial sites and date from prehistoric times. Legananny dolmen is on the slope to the west of little Boley Lough, which is about 6 miles outside Castlewellan. The model's identity is unknown but she serves a useful purpose in emphasising the scale of the dolmen. One wonders if our own monuments will last as long.

SOURCES

In research for this book the publications of the Ulster Architectural Heritage Society were extremely valuable. The relevant volumes are *Moira Rural District* (Belfast, 1969); *Mid Down* (Belfast, 1974); *Rathfriland and Hilltown* (Belfast, 1979). Other useful publications include *History of Saintfield and District* (Saintfield, 1971) Aitken McClelland; *County Down 100 years ago: a guide and directory 1886* (Dublin, 1886; reprinted Belfast, 1988) G. H. Bassett; *A history of the County of Down* (Dublin, 1875) A. Knox; *Walk about Saintfield* (Downpatrick, 1985) E. Minnis and C. Rogers; *Saintfield heritage* (Newcastle, 1982) ed. Saintfield Heritage Society; *A ramble through Dromore* (Belfast, 1886) John F. Mulligan; *Official guide of the Co.Down tourist district* (Belfast, 1898) R. L. Praeger; *The town in Ulster* (Belfast, 1951) Gilbert Camblin; *A history of Irish linen* (Belfast, 1971) D. G. McCrea; *Ballynahinch: centre of Down* (Ballynahinch, 1968) S. McCullough; *Hillsborough* (Belfast, 1962) John Barry; *Shaw's Tourist's picturesque guide to Carlingford Bay and the County Down* (London, 1877); *An historical account of the Diocese of Down and Connor: ancient and modern* (Vol 1, Dublin 1878) James O'Laverty; *Irish historical statistics: population 1921-71* (Dublin, 1978) ed. W. E. Vaughan and A. J. Fitzpatrick; *Topographical dictionary of Ireland* (2nd edition, Dublin, 1846) Samuel Lewis; *In praise of Ulster* (Belfast, 1938) Richard Hayward; *Ulster for your holidays* (Belfast, 1928) Ulster Tourist Development Association Limited; *Ulster for your holiday* (Belfast, 1936) Ulster Tourist Development Association Limited; *Black's Picturesque tourist of Ireland* (Edinburgh, 1866) *Tours in Ulster: a hand book to the Antiquities and Scenery of the North of Ireland* (Dublin, 1855) J. B. Doyle; *Letters from Georgian Ireland: the correspondence of Mary Delany 1731-68* (Belfast, 1991) ed. Angélique Day: *Buildings of Belfast* (Belfast, 1985) C. E. B. Brett; *Recollections of an Ulster Archdeacon* (Belfast, 1934) Rev. E. D. Atkinson; *Six generations of Friends in Ireland 1655-1890* (London, 1894) J. M. Richardson; *Ships and quaysides of Ulster* (Belfast, 1990) Robert Anderson and Ian Wilson; *Newry, Warrenpoint and Rostrevor* (Belfast, 1989) Fergus Hanna Bell; *Industrial archaeology of Co. Down* (Belfast, 1963) E. R. R. Green and the Belfast Newsletter *Ulster towns directories* for 1901 and 1921.

ACKNOWLEDGEMENTS

The photographs in this book are reproduced by kind permission of the trustees of the Ulster Folk and Transport Museum. My grateful thanks go to Ken Anderson and the photography department at the museum; also to both Ronnie Adams and Sally Skilling in the museum library who provided me with much help and encouragement. I would like to thank Brian M. Walker and Margaret McNulty of Friar's Bush Press for their encouragement and constructive criticism. I wish to acknowledge the following people for their assistance during the course of my research: the staff of the Newspaper Library in the Central Library, Belfast; the staff of the Linen Hall Library, Belfast; Miss Edna Young; Michael McCaughan of the Ulster Folk & Transport Museum; and finally R. Lyle for his encouragement.

Other photographs from the W A Green collection for this area not included in this selection.

Prints of these, and the photographs in the book, may be obtained from the photographic department of the Ulster Folk and Transport Museum, Cultra, Co Down.

WAG	16	Cromleac, Co Down
WAG	25A	Cromleac, Castlewellan
WAG	26	Loughinisland Lake, Downpatrick
WAG	27	Loughinisland Church, Co Down
WAG	27A	Loughinisland, Co Down
WAG	39	Cyclopean Door, Killeavy Abbey, Newry
WAG	40	Killeavy Abbey, Newry
WAG	48	The Butterlump, Strangford Lough
WAG	307	Narrowwater, Warrenpoint
WAG	308	Narrowwater, Warrenpoint
WAG	309	Old Cross, Kilbroney
WAG	311	Incised Cross, Kilbroney
WAG	312	Burren Cromleac, Warrenpoint
WAG	313	Standing Stone, Warrenpoint
WAG	315	Hotel and Promenade, Warrenpoint
WAG	317	Bathing Pavilion, Warrenpoint
WAG	561	Maghera Church of Ireland church
WAG	562	Maghera Round Tower
WAG	639	The Mount, Dromore
WAG	642	Castlewellan Castle
WAG	643	Castlewellan Castle
WAG	649	Dolly's Brae, Castlewellan
WAG	650	Magheralin Old Church
WAG	802	The Mount, Donaghmore, Newry
WAG	803	Donaghmore Cross, Newry
WAG	809	The Fairy Glen, Rostrevor
WAG	1010	Hand Warping for Damask Handloom weaving, Waringstown
WAG	1070	Handloom-weaving, Walpole Bros, Waringstown
WAG	1298	Hillsborough, Co Down
WAG	1299	The Market Place, Hillsborough
WAG	1433	Souterrain, Ballymagreehan, Castlewellan
WAG	1434	Stone Cashel, Loughislandreavy, Co. Down
WAG	1441	Rostrevor Mountain
WAG	1691	Donaghmore Old Cross
WAG	1692	Loughbrickland Lake and Crannoge
WAG	1709	Lough, Castlewellan
WAG	1783	Old Mill, Maghera
WAG	1783A	Old Mill, Maghera
WAG	1832	Altnadua, Castlewellan
WAG	1885	Loughislandreevy, Castlewellan
WAG	2032	The Obelisk, Rostrevor
WAG	2032A	The Obelisk, Rostrevor
WAG	2033	The Fairy Glen, Rostrevor
WAG	2033A	The Fairy Glen, Rostrevor
WAG	2033B	Rostrevor Mountain
WAG	2034	The Beach, Rostrevor
WAG	2036	G. N. R. Hotel, Rostrevor
WAG	2038	Narrowwater, Warrenpoint
WAG	2039	Narrowwater, Warrenpoint
WAG	2040	Rostrevor
WAG	2041A	Warrenpoint
WAG	2041B	Warrenpoint
WAG	2041C	Warrenpoint
WAG	2041D	Warrenpoint
WAG	2073	Edentubber Mountains
WAG	2467	Hillsborough Square & Market House
WAG	2470	Government House, Hillsborough
WAG	2472	Government House, Hillsborough
WAG	2473	The Temple from Government House, Hillsborough

WAG 2474 Waterfall in the grounds of Government House, Hillsborough
WAG 2475 Lake in grounds of Government House, Hillsborough
WAG 2476 Lake in grounds of Government House, Hillsborough
WAG 2478 Dane's cast, Scarva
WAG 2478A Dane's cast, Scarva
WAG 2481 Clanrye River & Bridge, Newry
WAG 2483 The Bann weir
WAG 2637 Rostrevor Mountain and Obilisk
WAG 2639 Woodside, Rostrevor
WAG 2640 Woodside, Rostrevor
WAG 2642 Rostrevor Mountain
WAG 2643 Fairy Glen, Rostrevor
WAG 2644 In the Fairy Glen, Rostrevor
WAG 2646A Clonallon Church, near Warrenpoint
WAG 2650 Carlingford Lough and Warrenpoint from Ferry Hill
WAG 2653 Halls Castle, Narrowwater, Co Down
WAG 2658 Castlewellan Castle, Co Down
WAG 2658A Castlewellan Castle, Co Down
WAG 2660 Carrickmannon Lake, Saintfield
WAG 2691 Carlingford Mountain and Lough from above Killowen
WAG 2692 The Neb of Killowen and Killowen village, Co Down
WAG 2697 Bellevue, Lurgan
WAG 2698A Ballynahinch, Co Down
WAG 2700 Slieve Croob from the Spa, Ballynahinch
WAG 2726 Banbridge, Co Down
WAG 2727A Solitude, Banbridge
WAG 2733 The River Bann at Hilltown
WAG 2733A The River Bann at Hiltown
WAG 3051 Loughislandreavy, Co Down

WAG 3052 Loughislandreavy, Co Down
WAG 3053 Loughislandreavy, Co Down
WAG 3080 Mourne Mountains above Kilbroney, Rostrevor
WAG 3125 Dolly's Brae
WAG 3126 Castlewellan
WAG 3129 Narrowwater castle
WAG 3130 Donaghmore Cross, Newry
WAG 3132 Ross Monument
WAG 3133 Rostrevor Square
WAG 3114 Fairy Glen, Rostrevor
WAG 3466 Killeavy Abbey, Newry
WAG 3587 A Paramoodra, Magheralin Quarry, Moira
WAG 3848 Trap, Old Castle, Hillsborough